This craft Notebook Belongs to

_____

_____

_____

Contact Details

_____

_____

_____

DEDICATION

This Crafters Journal is dedicated to all the crafters out there who want to track their craft projects and document their findings in the process.

You are my inspiration for producing books and I'm honored to be a part of keeping all of your Crafting notes and records organized.

This journal notebook will help you record your details about tracking your craft projects.

Thoughtfully put together with these sections to record: Project Name, Deadline, Description, Schedule, Resources, Notes, Supplies, and Tasks.

HOW TO USE THIS BOOK

The purpose of this book is to keep all of your Crafters notes all in one place. It will help keep you organized.

This Crafters Journal will allow you to accurately document every detail about your craft projects. It's a great way to chart your course through tracking your craft projects.

Here are examples of the prompts for you to fill in and write about your experience in this book:

1. Project Name

2. Deadline

3. Description

4. Schedule

5. Resources

6. Notes

7. Supplies

8. Tasks

CRAFT PROJECT PLANNER   PROJECT NAME: DEADLINE:

DESCRIPTION

SUPPLIES

SCHEDULE

RESOURCES

TASKS

NOTES

NOTES

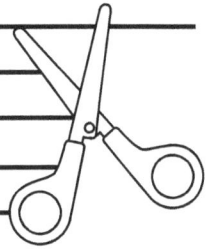

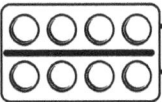

CRAFT PROJECT PLANNER   PROJECT NAME: DEADLINE:

DESCRIPTION

SUPPLIES

SCHEDULE

RESOURCES

TASKS

NOTES

NOTES

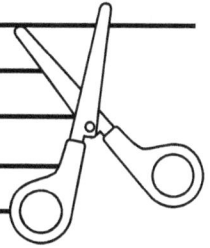

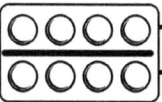

CRAFT PROJECT PLANNER   PROJECT NAME: DEADLINE:

DESCRIPTION

SUPPLIES

SCHEDULE

RESOURCES

TASKS

NOTES

NOTES

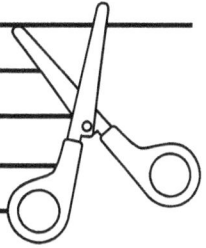

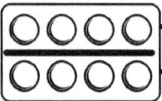

CRAFT PROJECT PLANNER   PROJECT NAME: DEADLINE:

DESCRIPTION

SUPPLIES

SCHEDULE

RESOURCES

TASKS

NOTES

NOTES

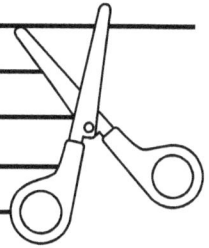

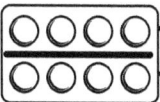

CRAFT PROJECT PLANNER   PROJECT NAME: DEADLINE:

DESCRIPTION

SUPPLIES

SCHEDULE

RESOURCES

TASKS

NOTES

NOTES

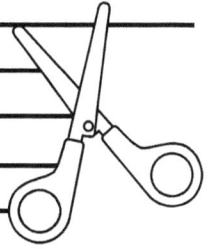

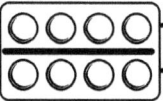

CRAFT PROJECT PLANNER   PROJECT NAME: DEADLINE:

DESCRIPTION

SUPPLIES

SCHEDULE

RESOURCES

TASKS

NOTES

NOTES

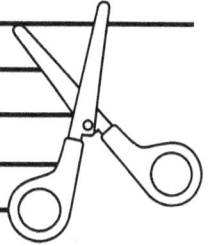

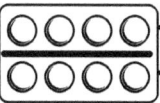

CRAFT PROJECT PLANNER   PROJECT NAME: DEADLINE:

DESCRIPTION

SUPPLIES

SCHEDULE

RESOURCES

TASKS

NOTES

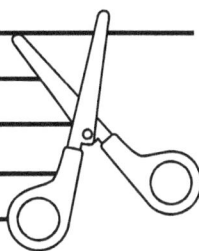

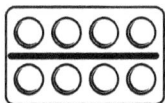

CRAFT PROJECT PLANNER   PROJECT NAME: DEADLINE:

DESCRIPTION

SUPPLIES

SCHEDULE

RESOURCES

TASKS

NOTES

NOTES

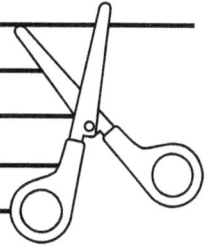

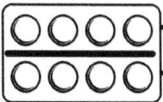

CRAFT PROJECT PLANNER   PROJECT NAME: DEADLINE:

DESCRIPTION

SUPPLIES

SCHEDULE

RESOURCES

TASKS

NOTES

NOTES

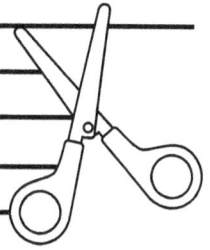

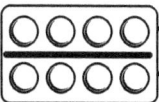

CRAFT PROJECT PLANNER   PROJECT NAME: DEADLINE:

DESCRIPTION

SUPPLIES

SCHEDULE

RESOURCES

TASKS

NOTES

NOTES

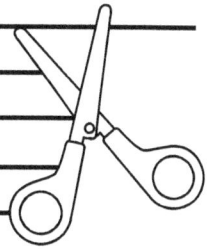

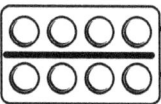

CRAFT PROJECT PLANNER   PROJECT NAME: DEADLINE:

DESCRIPTION

SUPPLIES

SCHEDULE

RESOURCES

TASKS

NOTES

NOTES

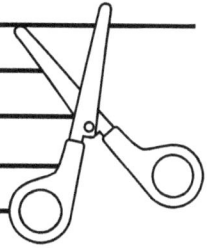

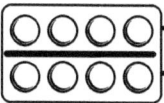

CRAFT PROJECT PLANNER   PROJECT NAME: DEADLINE:

DESCRIPTION

SUPPLIES

SCHEDULE

RESOURCES

TASKS

NOTES

NOTES

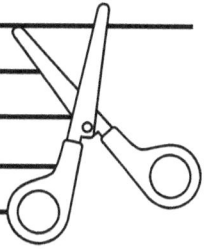

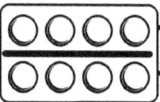

CRAFT PROJECT PLANNER   PROJECT NAME: DEADLINE:

DESCRIPTION

SUPPLIES

SCHEDULE

RESOURCES

TASKS

NOTES

NOTES

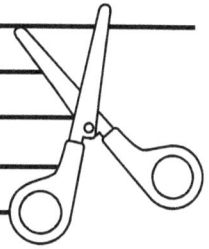
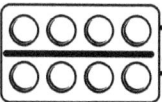

CRAFT PROJECT PLANNER   PROJECT NAME: DEADLINE:

DESCRIPTION

SUPPLIES

SCHEDULE

RESOURCES

TASKS

NOTES

NOTES

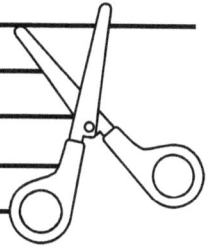

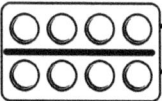

CRAFT PROJECT PLANNER   PROJECT NAME: DEADLINE:

DESCRIPTION

SUPPLIES

SCHEDULE

RESOURCES

TASKS

NOTES

NOTES

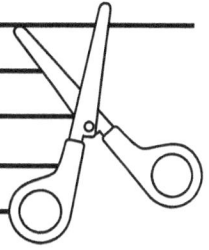

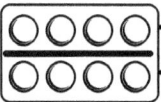

CRAFT PROJECT PLANNER   PROJECT NAME: DEADLINE:

DESCRIPTION

SUPPLIES

SCHEDULE

RESOURCES

TASKS

NOTES

NOTES

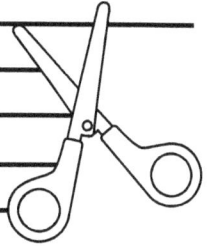
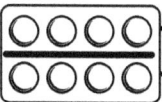

CRAFT PROJECT PLANNER   PROJECT NAME: DEADLINE:

DESCRIPTION

SCHEDULE

RESOURCES

NOTES

SUPPLIES

TASKS

NOTES

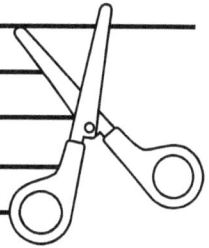

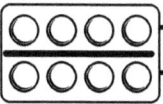

CRAFT PROJECT PLANNER   PROJECT NAME: DEADLINE:

DESCRIPTION

SUPPLIES

SCHEDULE

RESOURCES

TASKS

NOTES

NOTES

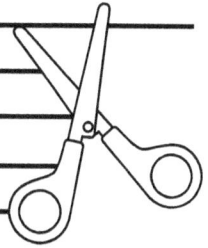

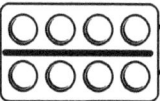

CRAFT PROJECT PLANNER   PROJECT NAME: DEADLINE:

DESCRIPTION

SUPPLIES

SCHEDULE

RESOURCES

TASKS

NOTES

NOTES

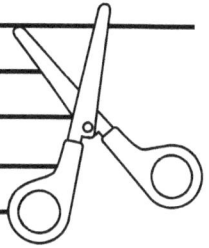

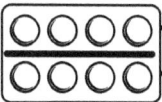

CRAFT PROJECT PLANNER   PROJECT NAME: DEADLINE:

DESCRIPTION

SUPPLIES

SCHEDULE

RESOURCES

TASKS

NOTES

NOTES

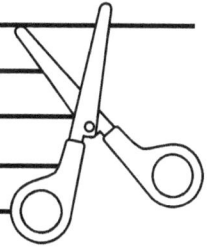

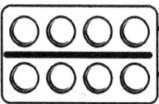

CRAFT PROJECT PLANNER   PROJECT NAME: DEADLINE:

DESCRIPTION

SUPPLIES

SCHEDULE

RESOURCES

TASKS

NOTES

NOTES

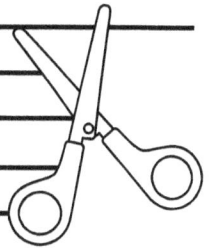

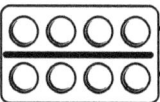

CRAFT PROJECT PLANNER   PROJECT NAME: DEADLINE:

DESCRIPTION

SUPPLIES

SCHEDULE

RESOURCES

TASKS

NOTES

NOTES

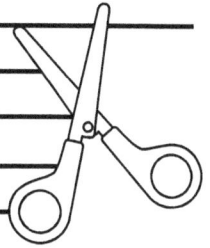

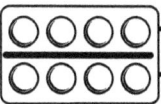

CRAFT PROJECT PLANNER   PROJECT NAME: DEADLINE:

DESCRIPTION

SUPPLIES

SCHEDULE

RESOURCES

TASKS

NOTES

NOTES

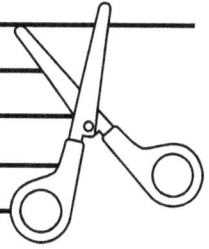

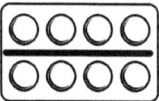

CRAFT PROJECT PLANNER   PROJECT NAME: DEADLINE:

DESCRIPTION

SUPPLIES

SCHEDULE

RESOURCES

TASKS

NOTES

NOTES

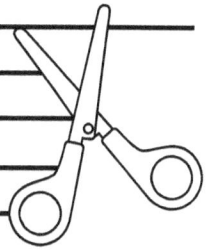

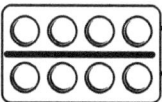

CRAFT PROJECT PLANNER   PROJECT NAME: DEADLINE:

DESCRIPTION

SUPPLIES

SCHEDULE

RESOURCES

TASKS

NOTES

NOTES

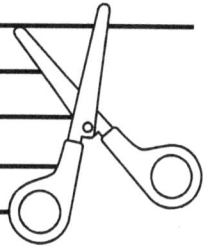

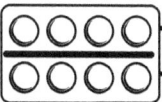

CRAFT PROJECT PLANNER   PROJECT NAME: DEADLINE:

DESCRIPTION

SUPPLIES

SCHEDULE

RESOURCES

TASKS

NOTES

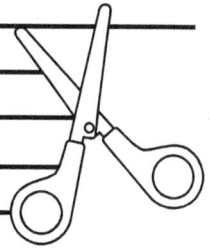

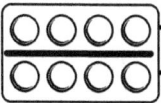

CRAFT PROJECT PLANNER   PROJECT NAME: DEADLINE:

DESCRIPTION

SUPPLIES

SCHEDULE

RESOURCES

TASKS

NOTES

NOTES

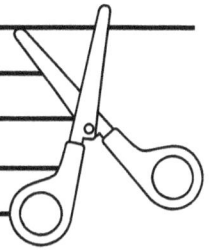

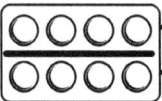

CRAFT PROJECT PLANNER   PROJECT NAME: DEADLINE:

DESCRIPTION

SUPPLIES

SCHEDULE

RESOURCES

TASKS

NOTES

NOTES

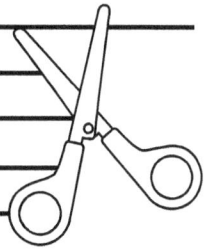

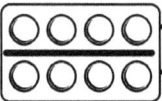

CRAFT PROJECT PLANNER   PROJECT NAME: DEADLINE:

DESCRIPTION

SUPPLIES

SCHEDULE

RESOURCES

TASKS

NOTES

NOTES

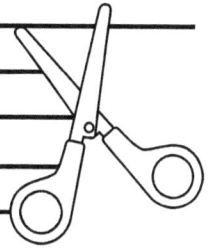

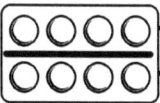

CRAFT PROJECT PLANNER   PROJECT NAME: DEADLINE:

DESCRIPTION

SUPPLIES

SCHEDULE

RESOURCES

TASKS

NOTES

NOTES

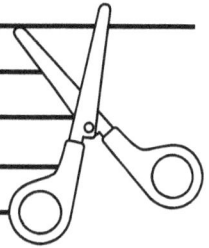
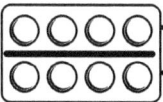

CRAFT PROJECT PLANNER   PROJECT NAME: DEADLINE:

DESCRIPTION

SUPPLIES

SCHEDULE

RESOURCES

TASKS

NOTES

NOTES

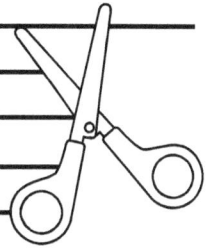

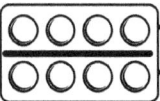

CRAFT PROJECT PLANNER   PROJECT NAME: DEADLINE:

DESCRIPTION

SUPPLIES

SCHEDULE

RESOURCES

TASKS

NOTES

NOTES

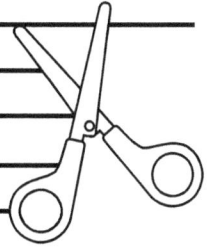

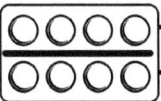

CRAFT PROJECT PLANNER   PROJECT NAME: DEADLINE:

DESCRIPTION

SUPPLIES

SCHEDULE

RESOURCES

TASKS

NOTES

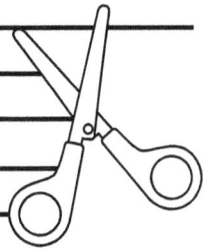

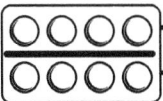

CRAFT PROJECT PLANNER   PROJECT NAME: DEADLINE:

DESCRIPTION

SUPPLIES

SCHEDULE

RESOURCES

TASKS

NOTES

NOTES

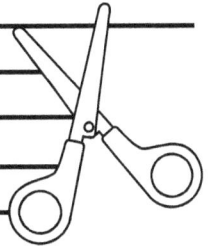

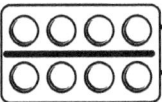

CRAFT PROJECT PLANNER   PROJECT NAME: DEADLINE:

DESCRIPTION

SUPPLIES

SCHEDULE

RESOURCES

TASKS

NOTES

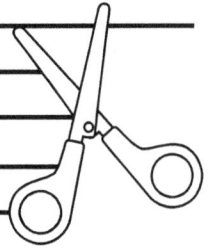

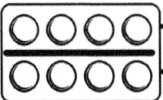

CRAFT PROJECT PLANNER   PROJECT NAME: DEADLINE:

DESCRIPTION

SUPPLIES

SCHEDULE

RESOURCES

TASKS

NOTES

NOTES

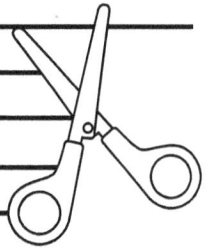

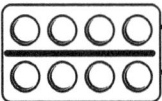

CRAFT PROJECT PLANNER   PROJECT NAME: DEADLINE:

DESCRIPTION

SUPPLIES

SCHEDULE

RESOURCES

TASKS

NOTES

NOTES

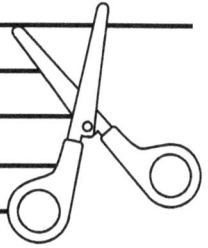

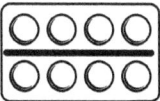

CRAFT PROJECT PLANNER   PROJECT NAME: DEADLINE:

DESCRIPTION

SUPPLIES

SCHEDULE

RESOURCES

TASKS

NOTES

NOTES

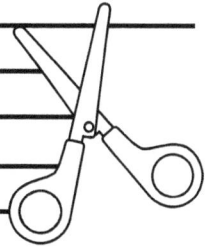

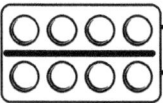

CRAFT PROJECT PLANNER   PROJECT NAME: DEADLINE:

DESCRIPTION

SUPPLIES

SCHEDULE

RESOURCES

TASKS

NOTES

NOTES

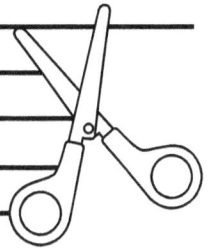

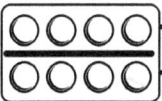

CRAFT PROJECT PLANNER   PROJECT NAME: DEADLINE:

DESCRIPTION

SUPPLIES

SCHEDULE

RESOURCES

TASKS

NOTES

NOTES

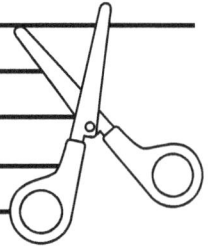

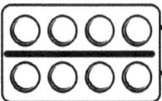